The Life and Work of...

Rembrandt van Rijn

Jayne Woodhouse

Heinemann Library
Chicago, Illinois

Designed by Celia Floyd
Illustrations by Sam Thompson
Originated by Ambassador Litho Ltd.
Printed and bound in Hong Kong/China

06 05 04 03
10 9 8 7 6 5 4 3 2

Library of Congress Cataloging-in-Publication Data
Woodhouse, Jayne, 1952-
  Rembrandt van Rijn / Jayne Woodhouse.
      p. cm. -- (The life and work of ...)
Includes bibliographical references and index.
Summary: Presents a brief overview of the life and work of this seventeenth-century Dutch painter, describing and giving examples of his work.
  ISBN 1-58810-606-3 (lib. bdg.)   ISBN 1-4034-0005-9 (pbk. bdg.)
  1. Rembrandt Harmenszoon van Rijn, 1606-1669--Juvenile literature. 2. Painters--Netherlands--Biography--Juvenile literature. [1. Rembrandt Harmenszoon van Rijn, 1606-1669. 2. Artists. 3. Painting, Dutch.] I. Title. II. Series.
  ND653.R4 W59 2002
  759.9492--dc21
                         2001003971

Acknowledgments
The author and publishers are grateful to the following for permission to reproduce copyright material:
pp. 4, 5, The National Gallery; p. 6, University of Leiden; pp. 7, 21, AKG London; pp. 8, 29, Hertzog Anton Ulrich Museum; p. 9, Musée des Beaux-Arts; p. 10, Hessisches Landesmuseum Darmstadt; p. 11, Royal Cabinet of Paintings/Mauritshuis/The Hague; p. 13, National Museum, Stockholm; p. 14, Giraudon/Bridgeman Art Library; p. 15, The Frick Collection; p. 17, Photographie Giraudon; p. 19, Museum Boymans van Beuningen, p. 23, Rotterdam; Bridgeman Art Library; p. 25, The National Gallery, London; p. 27, AKG London/Louvre, Paris.

Cover photograph reproduced with permission of AKG London.

Special thanks to Katie Miller for her comments in the preparation of this book.

Every effort has been made to contact copyright holders of any material reproduced in this book. Any omissions will be rectified in subsequent printings if notice is given to the publisher.

Some words are shown in bold, **like this.** You can find out what they mean by looking in the glossary.

Contents

Who Was Rembrandt?

Rembrandt van Rijn was one of the greatest artists of all time. He signed hundreds of his paintings and drawings with just his first name. Many of these are **masterpieces** of art.

Rembrandt did over 100 paintings of himself.
They give us clues about what his life was like.
He painted this **self-portrait** when he was 34.
He was already famous by then.

Self-Portrait, 1640

Early Life

Rembrandt was born on July 15, 1606, in Leiden, Holland. He had eight brothers and sisters. His father was a **miller.** He worked in one of the windmills shown on this map of Leiden.

Rembrandt did many **portraits** of his parents.
He made this **etching** of his mother when he
was 25, the year after his father died.

Rembrandt's Mother with a Black Shawl, 1631

Learning to Be an Artist

When he was fifteen, Rembrandt began to study art. First, he studied near his home. Then he began studying in **Amsterdam.** One of his teachers, Pieter Lastman, painted this picture.

David in the Temple, 1618, by Pieter Lastman

This is the first known work by Rembrandt. He painted it when he was nineteen. It is a scene from the Bible. Look carefully behind the kneeling figure. Do you see Rembrandt's face?

The Stoning of St. Stephen, 1625

Early Works

In 1625, Rembrandt returned to Leiden and opened his own **studio.** He began teaching art. This is a drawing of Rembrandt's studio by one of his students. It was a very busy place.

Rembrandt painted more Bible scenes. He was very good at showing light and shadow in his pictures. In this oil painting, it looks as if a bright light is shining on baby Jesus.

Presentation of Jesus in the Temple, 1631

11

Everyday People

In Rembrandt's time, most artists only painted important people. Rembrandt took his **sketchbook** with him to walk through town. He **sketched** older people, workers, and **beggars** that he saw.

12

Simeon in the Temple, 1666–69

Rembrandt used some of these drawings of everyday people as **models** for his Bible scenes. The face of this old man is much like someone Rembrandt had sketched in town.

A Famous Portrait Painter

When Rembrandt was 25, he moved to **Amsterdam**. There were many wealthy people living there. Many of them wanted to have paintings of themselves and their families.

Rembrandt was soon given his first **commission**. Nicolaes Ruts, a rich **merchant,** paid Rembrandt to paint this **portrait** of him. Rembrandt's work was very popular. Over the next few years, he painted almost 50 portraits.

Nicolaes Ruts,
1631

Marriage and Success

In 1634, Rembrandt married Saskia van Uylenburgh. She was a rich, young woman. Later, they moved to this grand house. Rembrandt filled the house with his paintings.

Saskia van Uylenburgh, 1634

Rembrandt and Saskia were very happy at first. Rembrandt painted his wife in many different **costumes.** In this **portrait,** she is wearing rich clothes and jewels.

Rembrandt's Children

Sadly, Rembrandt and Saskia's happiness did not last very long. Their first child lived only two months. Their next two children also died when they were just babies.

In 1641, they had a son named Titus. When Titus was fourteen, Rembrandt painted this **portrait** of him sitting at his desk. Titus looks like he is deep in thought.

Titus at his Desk, 1655

The Artist Alone

In 1642, when Titus was just nine months old, Saskia became ill and died. She was only 30. Rembrandt was left alone with his young son.

The Company of Captain F.B. Cocq (The Night Watch), 1642

In the same year, Rembrandt finished his most famous picture. It is known as *The Night Watch*. It shows the town guardsmen going to work. Rembrandt used movement, light, and shadow to bring the scene to life.

Landscapes

Rembrandt stopped painting quite as many of the **portraits** for which he was famous. He spent hours walking alone in the countryside. He sometimes made **sketches** of the places he saw.

Rembrandt drew this winter scene using an ink pen. He created a cold **landscape** with just a few strokes of the pen. He left much of the paper blank.

Winter Landscape with Cottages Among Trees, about 1650

A New Life

When Rembrandt was about 40, he fell in love with his young servant, Hendrickje Stoffels. They later had a daughter named Cornelia. Rembrandt often **sketched** his family life.

Rembrandt's new happiness led to some of his greatest paintings. Hendrickje was the **model** for this woman bathing in a stream.

Hendrickje Bathing, 1654

Troubled Times

Rembrandt was spending a lot of money and soon could not pay his bills. In 1658, he had to sell everything he owned. Within the next ten years, Hendrickje and Titus both died.

Rembrandt never stopped painting. He finished this **self-portrait** when he was nearly 60. He is holding his **palette** and brushes and wearing his work clothes. He seems to be telling us that he is still an artist in spite of all he has lost.

Self-Portrait,
about 1665

Rembrandt Dies

Rembrandt died on October 4, 1669. He was 63. He was buried in the same church as Hendrickje and Titus. Today, Rembrandt's works can be seen in art **galleries** all over the world.

This **portrait** is one of Rembrandt's last paintings. He never finished it. No one knows who these people were. Perhaps Rembrandt was thinking about the family he had lost.

Family Portrait, 1668–69

Timeline

1606	Rembrandt van Rijn is born in Leiden, Holland, on July 15.
1620	Rembrandt attends Leiden University.
1624	He moves to **Amsterdam** to study with the famous artist Pieter Lastman.
1625	Rembrandt returns to Leiden and sets up his own **studio.**
1631	He makes his home in Amsterdam.
1634	He marries Saskia van Uylenburgh.
1639	Rembrandt and Saskia buy a new home at Number 4, Breestraat.
1641	Their son, Titus, is born.
1642	Saskia dies.
1647	Around this time, Rembrandt and his servant, Hendrickje Stoffels, live together as a married couple. She is 20 years younger than Rembrandt.
1654	Rembrandt and Hendrickje have a daughter, Cornelia.
1657	Rembrandt begins to sell off his belongings.
1658	His house is sold because he cannot pay his bills.
1663	Hendrickje dies.
1668	Rembrandt's only son, Titus, dies.
1669	Rembrandt dies on October 4 at the age of 63.

Glossary

Amsterdam capital city of Holland, or the Netherlands

beggar poor or homeless person who asks for money

commission being asked to make a piece of art

costume clothes that are borrowed for dressing-up

etching picture scratched into a metal plate

gallery room or building where works of art are shown

landscape picture of the countryside

masterpiece great work of art by a famous artist

merchant someone who buys and sells goods to foreign countries

miller someone who works at a mill

model person who poses for an artist to draw or paint

palette flat piece of wood on which an artist mixes paint

portrait painting of a person

self-portrait picture an artist makes of himself or herself

sketch unfinished or rough drawing or painting

sketchbook notepad in which an artist makes rough drawings

studio room or building where an artist works

Index

More Books to Read

de Bie, Ceciel. *Rembrandt*. Los Angeles: Getty Publications, 2001.

Spence, David. *Rembrandt*. Hauppauge, N.Y.: Barron's, 1997.

Venezia, Mike. *Rembrandt*. Danbury, Conn.: Children's Press, 1988.

More Artwork to See

Old Man with a Gold Chain. About 1631. The Art Institute of Chicago, Illinois.

Portrait of Christ. About 1655–57. Hyde Collection Art Museum, Glens Falls, N.Y.

Woman with a Pink. Early 1600s. Metropolitan Museum of Art, New York, N.Y.